A Guide for Using

Stone Soup

in the Classroom

Based on the book written by Marcia Brown

D1543793

*This guide written by **Susan Onion***

Teacher Created Materials, Inc.
6421 Industry Way
Westminster, CA 92683
www.teachercreated.com
©2000 Teacher Created Materials
Reprinted, 2003
Made in U.S.A.
ISBN 0-7439-3005-3

Edited by
Gisela Lee
Illustrated by
Wendy Chang
Cover Art by
Wendy Chang

Table of Contents

Introduction

A good book can touch the lives of children like a good friend. Marcia Brown has brought to life such a story in her humorous retelling of the French folk tale, *Stone Soup*. Great care was taken in selecting the books and activities featured in the Literature Unit series. All activities are intended for use with primary students, grades 1–3. Some activities may need to be modified to meet the needs of students at various levels of ability. (Several modification options are included in Suggestions for Using the Unit Activities, pages 7–11.) Activities in all academic subjects have been incorporated to make this a unit that teaches and reinforces skills across the curriculum. It is hoped that students will enjoy the story while gaining knowledge and skills in all areas.

A Sample Lesson Plan

The Sample Lesson Plan on page 4 provides you with a specific set of lesson plan suggestions. Each of the lessons can take from one to several days to complete and can include all or some of the suggested activities. Refer to the Suggestions for Using the Unit Activities on pages 7–11 for information relating to the unit activities.

A Unit Planner

If you wish to tailor the suggestions on pages 7–11 to a format other than the one prescribed in the Sample Lesson Plan, a blank Unit Planner is provided on page 5. Plan each day on this sheet by writing the activity numbers or brief notations about the lessons that you wish to accomplish. Space has been provided for reminders, comments, and other pertinent information related to each day's activities. Reproduce copies of the Unit Planner as needed.

Sample Lesson Plan

Lesson 1

- Introduce the unit by using any or all of the Before the Book activities (page 7).
- Share information from About the Author (page 6) with the students to learn interesting facts about Marcia Brown.
- Introduce the vocabulary (page 16).
- Read the story for enjoyment.
- Discuss some of the story questions (page 15).

Lesson 2

- Reread the story to the class or have students read the story aloud with a partner.
- Complete the Ten Important Sentences activity (page 22).
- Continue vocabulary activities (page 16).
- Continue discussing the story questions (page 15).
- Have students plan their own imaginary soups (page 25).
- Learn about the sense of smell by completing the experiment on page 37.

Lesson 3

- Discuss setting, characters, problem, and solution by organizing the story (page 23).
- Work on problem solving skills by solving Soup Problems (page 32).
- Discuss healthy foods and diets (pages 35 and 36).
- Practice writing skills and foster creativity with a writing activity (page 21).
- Learn about the art of oral storytelling. Complete the activities on page 30.

Lesson 4

- Compare and contrast the main characters (page 24).
- Learn about synonyms and antonyms (page 27).
- Work with a partner to create a counting book in French (page 33).
- Complete Fraction Fun (page 31).
- Learn about the sense of taste by completing the experiments on pages 38 and 39.
- Make peasant bonnets and soldier hats (pages 40 and 41).

Lesson 5

- Reread the story. Work together to create a Reader's Theater Script (page 20).
- Work in groups to make stick puppet theaters and stick puppets (pages 17–19).
- Complete the Best Beds activity (page 29).
- Work with a partner to complete the Strange Words activity (page 26).
- Learn a French folk song and folk dance (pages 42 and 43).
- Complete "What Do You Think?" (page 28).

Lesson 6

- Complete Graphing Ingredients (page 34).
- Work in groups to write recipes. Then, make stone soup (pages 44 and 45).
- Present the reader's theater, the folk song, and the folk dance before an audience. Share stone soup at your celebration.
- Collect food for a local food bank (page 11).

Unit Planner

Unit Activities	
(Date)	
Notes/Comments:	

Unit Activities	
(Date)	
Notes/Comments:	

Unit Activities	
(Date)	
Notes/Comments:	

Unit Activities	
(Date)	
Notes/Comments:	

Unit Activities	
(Date)	
Notes/Comments:	

Unit Activities	
(Date)	
Notes/Comments:	

Getting to Know the Book and the Author

About the Book

Three soldiers are returning home from a war. They are very tired and hungry. As they are walking, they see a small village and decide to stop and ask for some food. But the peasants, who are greedy and do not wish to share their food with the hungry soldiers, decide to hide their food and claim that they have none to share. The soldiers talk and make a plan. The plan involves making soup from stones and tricking the villagers into sharing their stores. Soon there is a feast for all, and the villagers are thanking the clever soldiers for teaching them how to make stone soup.

About the Author

Marcia Brown was born on July 13, 1918, in Rochester, New York. Even as a child, she knew she loved art. She has memories of drawing on large pads of paper with her sisters and of drawing on the kitchen wall that her father painted so she could use it as a chalkboard. Reading was also very important to her family. She remembers reading for entertainment, and she recalls making frequent trips to the library as a child.

After graduating from New York College for Teachers (now University of New York at Albany), she taught high school English and drama, but she knew that she wanted to be an artist. So she left teaching and moved to New York City, where she took a job as a librarian. There she learned about storytelling and children's literature. She wrote her first book, *The Little Carousel*, which was published in 1946. Her second book was *Stone Soup*.

Marcia Brown uses many different mediums to illustrate her books. Some of the mediums she has used are painting, wood and tile printing, and photography. She feels that each book is an individual and therefore the art needs to reflect the character of the story.

Fairy tales and folk tales are especially important to Marcia Brown. As a child, she loved reading stories by Hans Christian Anderson and the Grimm Brothers. As an author, she believes in the importance of passing down folk tales from one generation to the next. Many of Marcia Brown's folk tales have been translated into other languages and have been published around the world.

Marcia Brown has produced over 30 children's books during her career. She has been awarded many prestigious awards, including three Caldecott Medals and six Honor Medals for the outstanding children's picture book of the year. She is also a recipient of the Laura Ingalls Wilder Award for her lasting contribution to children's literature.

Suggestions for Using the Unit Activities

Use some or all of the following suggestions to introduce your students to *Stone Soup* and to expand their appreciation of the book through activities that cross the curriculum. The suggested activities have been divided into three sections to assist you in planning this literature unit.

Suggestions are arranged as follows:

- **Before the Book** includes suggestions for preparing the classroom environment and the students for the literature to be read.
- **Into the Book** has activities that focus on the book's content, characters, theme, etc.
- **After the Book** extends the readers' enjoyment of the book.

Before the Book

1. Before you begin the unit, prepare the vocabulary cards, story questions, and sentence strips for the pocket chart activities.

2. Stimulate prior knowledge through the following activities:
   - discussing what a recipe is
   - listing different kinds of soups
   - defining the words greedy and generous
     (A brief lesson on hard g and soft g could be included while discussing these two words.)
   - talking about what it feels like to be hungry and full
   - locating France on a map
   - asking students what they know about folk tales
   - discussing what it means to trick someone

3. Introduce vocabulary (page 16) to your students by doing any of the following:
   - Discuss the meanings of the words before reading the book.
   - Duplicate the vocabulary list on page 16 for each student. Read the words together orally. Students can cut out the words and make them into flashcards.
   - Make several copies of the soup pot pattern on page 14. Write the vocabulary words on the soup pots and display them in the pocket chart. (See page 12 for directions on making a pocket chart.)
   - Make a transparency of the vocabulary page and project it for the entire class to view.

4. Show students the book cover. Discuss the title and picture. Ask the students to make predictions about the story.

5. Share some of the information about the author from page 6. Ask students if they have read any other books by Marcia Brown and invite them to tell about these books.

Suggestions for Using the Unit Activities *(cont.)*

Into the Book

1. Language Arts

❑ *Reading the Story*

Read the story aloud to the class for enjoyment. Since Stone Soup is a folk tale and written with the art of oral storytelling in mind, the text lends itself well to a dramatic reading. Invite students to show you how the peasants pretended to look hungry and how their eyes would "grow round" with surprise. Incorporate voices for the soldiers and the peasants.

❑ *Story Questions (page 15)*

Develop critical thinking skills, using the story questions on page 15. The questions are based on Bloom's Taxonomy and are provided for each level of Bloom's Levels of Learning. Write the questions on the soup pot pattern or on sentence strips for display in the pocket chart. More ways to use the questions are suggested on page 13.

❑ *Journal and Creative Writing Ideas (page 21)*

Use this page to help students begin journal entries, write creative stories with partners or teams, or start off a writer's workshop session.

❑ *Ten Important Sentences (page 22)*

Discuss how a summary is a shortened version of a longer story. Ask students when someone might use a summary and why. Read the directions together. Then call on students to read the sentences on the page. Have students either work in pairs or independently to place the sentences in the correct order. Check work before gluing in place. Put sentences in order in the pocket chart or on an overhead.

❑ *Organize the Story (page 23)*

Review the words: character, setting, problem, and solution. Then read and follow the directions. Answers for problem and solution may vary. Students can also share their illustrations.

❑ *Comparing Characters (page 24)*

Read the directions, then have students work with partners to complete the Venn diagram. When teams are finished, bring the class together to share information. List ideas on a large diagram drawn on butcher paper or on the board.

❑ *Plan a Soup (page 25)*

Discuss the important parts of a recipe. Read the directions. Then brainstorm some ideas for soup starters. Have students complete the page independently and then share their soup creations. This activity can be modified to become a colorful bulletin board display by enlarging the soup pot and printing it on construction paper. Then have students draw or cut and paste their ingredients into the larger pot. Mount the recipe cards on the front of the soup pots for classmates to read.

Suggestions for Using the Unit Activities *(cont.)*

Into the Book *(cont.)*

1. Language Arts *(cont.)*

❏ *Strange Words (page 26)*

List some common expressions on the board, such as: fast as a rabbit, ate a ton, slow as molasses, or a busy beaver. Discuss what these words say and what they mean. Then read the directions for the activity. Have students work in teams to explain the unusual expressions from the story. When finished, compare and discuss answers. Follow up by discussing the questions at the bottom of the page.

❏ *Same or Different? (page 27)*

Review what antonyms and synonyms are; read the directions and have students complete the activity independently.

❏ *What Do You Think? (page 28)*

Discuss and define what an opinion is. Discuss the quote that is at the beginning of the page and ask students what they think about it. Have the students then answer the questions related to their interpretations of the quote and discuss their answers afterwards.

❏ *Best Beds (page 29)*

Read the directions at the top of the page. Ask the students why the baker, mayor, and priest had what were considered the best beds in the village. Brainstorm who might have the best beds in your town. Then have students complete the page and share ideas.

❏ *Folk Tales Anyone? (page 30)*

Choose some or all of the activities on this page to help your students experience the art of oral storytelling. You may wish to follow this activity with a visit from a guest storyteller.

2. Math

❏ *Fraction Fun (page 31)*

Review fractions with your students, then have them complete the fraction activity ndependently.

❏ *Soup Problems (page 32)*

Read the directions together, then solve the problems. You may have students work on this activity in teams, with partners, or independently. Modification: The math on this page can be simplified by reducing the two-digit numbers to single digits by writing out all of the 1's before copying.

Suggestions for Using the Unit Activities *(cont.)*

Into the Book *(cont.)*

2. Math *(cont.)*

❑ *Counting in French (page 33)*

Begin this activity by sharing some counting books with your class. (See the bibliography on page 47 for some titles.) Copy the French number chart onto an overhead or butcher paper, but do not display the chart. Say the numbers one at a time and have students repeat. After number 5, review and challenge some students to recite 1–5. Continue to 10. After challenging a few students to count from 1–10 in French, show the chart and have the entire class count together. Hand out the activity page to each student along with ten sheets ofpaper, preferably bound into a booklet. Have students write the numbers with their names in French on the pages. Then have students illustrate.

❑ *Graphing Ingredients (page 34)*

Read the directions and the information paragraph together. Then have students fill in the graph and answer the questions at the bottom.

3. Health

❑ *Healthy Foods (pages 35 and 36)*

Study the food pyramid with the class. Explain how we should eat more servings from the food groups at the base of the pyramid. Discuss the importance of a balanced diet. Have students answer the questions. Then attach the sheets together and send the packet home to complete as homework. A follow-up activity to this lesson is to split students into groups and assign each group a food group. Students work as a team to cut out pictures of foods that belong in their food group, then glue to tagboard to form a healthy food collage.

4. Science

❑ *Smells (page 37)*

Have students work in teams to complete these experiments. Read the directions, and hand out the samples. To prepare samples you will need paper cups, tissues, rubber bands, and various ingredients (listed below). Place the ingredients into a cup and cover with a tissue. Use the rubber band to secure the tissue around the cup. Prepare five samples for each group in your class. Some ingredient suggestions are: lemon juice/slice, cinnamon, molasses, peanut butter, vinegar, mustard, banana, garlic, onion, and chocolate syrup.

❑ *Tastes (pages 38 and 39)*

Discuss the sense of taste and how important it is to our daily lives. Explain that our sense of taste is influenced by both our nose and tongue. Then have your students complete these two taste experiments. Both of these experiments can be completed as a class or in a center. (**Note:** Check for possible food allergies before allowing students to participate.)

5. Art

❑ *Hat Patterns (pages 40 and 41)*

This is a great activity for listening to directions. Hand out materials and lead your class step by step in making the two hats. Although the boys may not wish to wear the bonnets, they can be encouraged to make one for a younger sister or friend.

Suggestions for Using the Unit Activities *(cont.)*

Into the Book *(cont.)*

6. Music/Social Studies/P. E.

❏ *French Folk Song (page 42)*

Teach your students this simple French folk song. A pronunciation key is available if you are unfamiliar with the language.

❏ *Folk Dance (page 43)*

After teaching your students the folk song, continue the lesson by learning the accompanying folk dance.

After the Book

Culminating Activities

❏ *Souper Supper (page 46)*

Send out the invitation on page 46 to parents or to another class, inviting them to come taste your stone soup and to share in your culminating presentations.

❏ *Let's Make Soup (page 44)*

Follow the lesson outline for having students write their own soup recipes. Then use the recipe guideline to make stone soup.

❏ *Writing a Recipe for Stone Soup (page 45)*

After discussing recipes, invite students to share one of their favorite recipes with the class. Send home a copy of the large recipe card on page 45 and ask students to write out one of their favorite recipes. Bind the recipes together to make a class book. A parent volunteer can type out the recipes and make copies so the entire class can take the recipes home.

❏ *Create a Reader's Theater Script (page 20)*

Develop a script to be performed reader's theater style. Provide a copy of the script for each performer. Highlight the parts and laminate the scripts before distributing them. In groups, students can choose or be assigned parts. Practice reading the script together. When the performers are ready to make a presentation to an audience, have them stand in a line or in a semicircle to perform. Students can wear the simple costumes suggested on page 20 or use their stick puppets to represent characters.

❏ *Collect Food for a Food Pantry*

Discuss how the soldiers were hungry and how they did not have any food. Then discuss how there are people in your own community who also may not have enough food. Invite students to bring in non-perishable goods to donate to a local food bank. If you are unable to locate a food pantry in your town, the national agencies listed on page 47 may be able to help you find a nearby resource.

Pocket Chart Activities

Prepare a pocket chart for storing and using vocabulary cards, story questions, and sentence strips.

How to Make a Pocket Chart

If a commercial pocket chart is unavailable, you can make a pocket chart if you have access to a laminator. Begin by laminating a 24" x 36" (61 cm x 91 cm) piece of colored tagboard. Cut nine 2" x 20" (5 cm x 51 cm) or six 3" x 20" (8 cm x 51 cm) strips of clear plastic to use as pockets. Space the strips equally down the 36" (91 cm) length of the tagboard. Attach each strip with clear, plastic tape along the sides and bottom. This will hold the sentence strips, word cards, etc., and can be displayed in a learning center or mounted on a chalk rail for use with a group.

How to Use a Pocket Chart

1. On light gray paper, reproduce the soup pot pattern on page 14. Make vocabulary cards as directed on page 7. Print the definitions on sentence strips for a matching activity.

definition or sentence   word

definition or sentence   word

definition or sentence   word

definition or sentence   word

definition or sentence   word

Pocket Chart Activities *(cont.)*

How to Use a Pocket Chart *(cont.)*

---

2. Print the ten important sentences from the story (page 22) on sentence strips, then have the students place them in sequential order in the pocket chart. This can be done as a class (to self check) after completing the activity on page 22 or as a center for small group work.

3. Make a set of cards with the different foods that were listed in the story. Have students group the food cards by their food groups, put food cards in alphabetical order, or use the food cards to rank their favorites.

4. Reproduce several copies of the soup pot pattern on page 14 in six different colors. Use a different color of the soup pot pattern to represent each level of Bloom's Levels of Learning.

For example:

I. Knowledge (red)

II. Comprehension (orange)

III. Application (yellow)

IV. Analysis (green)

V. Synthesis (blue)

VI. Evaluation (violet)

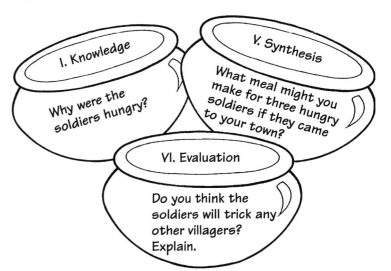

Write a story question from page 15 on the appropriate color-coded soup pot pattern. Write the level of the question and the question on the soup pot, as shown in the example.

5. After reading the story, use these questions to provide opportunities for students to develop and practice higher level, critical thinking skills.

- Use a specific color-coded set of cards to question students at a particular level of learning.

- Have a student choose a card and read it out loud or give it to the teacher to read aloud. Have the student answer the question or call on a volunteer to answer it.

- Arrange the students in pairs. Read a question and have partners take turns answering the question.

- Play a game. Divide the class into two teams. Mix up the question cards and then ask the team members to answer the question that is read. The teams will score one point for each appropriate answer.

Pocket Chart Patterns

Duplicate these patterns as needed for use with the pocket chart activities on pages 12 and 13. Enlarge or reduce the patterns to fit a particular activity.

Story Questions

Use the following questions with the suggested activities on page 13. Prepare the soup pot pattern on page 14 and write a different question on each pot.

I. KNOWLEDGE *(ability to recall information)*
- Why were the soldiers hungry?
- Where did the peasants hide their food?
- What did the soldiers put in the soup?
- Where did the soldiers sleep?

II. COMPREHENSION *(ability to master basic understanding of information)*
- Why did the peasants hide their food?
- How did the peasants react when the soldiers asked for food?
- Why were the peasants surprised when the soldiers announced that they would make stone soup?
- How did the soldiers trick the peasants?

III. APPLICATION *(ability to do something new with information)*
- What might have happened if the first family invited the soldiers in to eat?
- Do you think the peasants would feed the next strangers to visit their town?
- What ingredients would you put in stone soup?
- If the peasants make stone soup again, what do you think they will put into the pot?

IV. ANALYSIS *(ability to examine the parts of the whole)*
- Why do you think the peasants agreed to bring their hidden food to the soldiers?
- Why do you think the soldiers made enough soup for the entire village?
- Do you think the soldiers could have made their soup without using stones?
- What do you think the peasants learned from meeting the soldiers?

V. SYNTHESIS *(ability to bring together information to make something new)*
- What would have happened if the peasants did not go to their homes and bring back the ingredients for the soup?
- What meal might you make for three hungry soldiers if they came to your town?
- The soldiers slept in special places in the town. Where might you invite the soldiers to sleep for the night?

VI. EVALUATION *(ability to form and defend an opinion)*
- Do you think the soldiers were right to trick the peasants? Why or why not?
- Do you think the soldiers will trick any other villages? Explain.
- If you were a peasant, would you have welcomed the soldiers into your home? Why or why not?
- Do you think people should help other people who have no food and are hungry? Explain.

Vocabulary List

See page 7 for directions.

soldiers	cellars	roast
trudged	generally	torches
impossible	fetch	fancy
peasants	banquet	splendid
loft	broth	indeed
barley	require	gathered

Stick Puppet Theater

Make a class set of puppet theaters (one for each student) or make one theater for every two to four students. The patterns and directions for making the stick puppets are on pages 18 and 19.

Materials

- 24" x 36" (60 cm x 90 cm) pieces of colored poster board or cardboard (enough for each student or group of students)
- markers, crayons, or paints and paintbrushes
- scissors or a craft knife (knife is for adult use only)

Directions

1. Fold the poster board or cardboard about 8" (20 cm) in from each of the shorter sides.
2. Cut a "window" in the front panel, large enough to accommodate two or three stick puppets.
3. Let children personalize and decorate their own theaters.
4. Laminate the stick puppet theaters to make them more durable. You may wish to send the theaters home at the end of the year or save them to use year after year.

Suggestions for Using the Puppets and Theaters

- Prepare the stick puppets, using the directions on page 18. Use the puppets and the puppet theater with the reader's theater script developed from page 20. You may want to have students make "food puppets" by drawing pictures of the foods in the soup or by cutting out pictures from magazines and then mounting them on tagboard.
- Let the students experiment with the puppets by retelling the story in their own words or by reading from the book.
- Read the quote on page 28 and have the students hold up the character who is speaking.
- Have the students create new adventures for the soldiers as they go to the next village.

Stick Puppet Theater *(cont.)*

Directions: Reproduce the patterns on tagboard or construction paper. Have students color the patterns. Cut them along the dashed lines. To complete the stick puppets, glue each pattern to a tongue depressor or craft stick. Use the stick puppets with the puppet theater or as part of your culminating experience.

Stick Puppet Theater *(cont.)*

See page 18 for directions.

Create a Reader's Theater Script

Reader's theater is an exciting and easy method of providing students with the opportunity to perform a play while minimizing the use of props, sets, costumes, or memorization. Students read the dialogue of the characters or narrator from the book or a prepared script. The dialogue may be read from the book just as the author has written it, or the teacher and students may create a new script.

How to Create a Script

- Read through the book again with the students. Discuss story development, listing events on the board or on a large piece of paper. Have students establish events that represent the beginning, middle, and end of the story.

- Print and discuss examples of word patterns followed throughout the book. For example, the soldiers often say, "If we only had _____, the soup would be better."

Some other patterns you may wish to use:

- So _____ ran to fetch _____.

- " _____, can you spare a bit of food?"

- "We have no food," said _____.

- Use these word patterns to guide your students as they retell the story. Have students help you fill in the characters and important information to complete the script. (Older students may be encouraged to rephrase the word patterns as they develop the story.)

- On pages 18 and 19, pictures of soldiers and peasants have been provided for you to use with the puppet theater. These may be used with the script, or new characters may be chosen. If new characters are chosen, write their responses on the board, then incorporate them as needed into your script.

- Copy the new script so each student has his or her own copy.

- Encourage students to use sound effects and dramatic voices while reading the play.

How to Make Simple Costumes

Although costumes are not necessary in reader's theater productions, your students may wish to wear simple costumes. Here are some suggestions:

- Students can wear signs around their necks, indicating their speaking parts. Prepare signs by writing the name of the reader's character on a piece of construction paper. Staple or tape a piece of yarn to the top of the paper.

- Students can wear hats to represent their characters. Soldiers can wear hats made from paper (page 41). Peasant girls can wear paper bonnets (page 40) with shawls or aprons, while peasant boys can wear stocking caps or berets.

In a reader's theater production, everyone can be involved in some way. Encourage class members to participate in off-stage activities, such as greeting the audience and assisting behind the scenes.

Journal and Creative Writing Ideas

Here are some ideas you may wish to use in your journals or for other creative writing activities. You may be asked to write on your own or to complete a writing activity by working in pairs, small groups, or as a whole class.

- ◆ The soldiers arrive in the village and plan to make stone soup, but they cannot find any stones. What do they make instead?

- ◆ Instead of three soldiers, three hungry magicians come to town. What kind of soup would they make?

- ◆ What would you make for three hungry soldiers? Plan a meal that you might serve at your house.

- ◆ What happens when the peasants try to make stone soup after the soldiers are gone?

- ◆ As the soldiers are making stone soup, one of the peasants figures out that the soldiers are tricking them. What happens next?

- ◆ Imagine that you are a peasant in the story. Write a diary entry describing a day in your life.

- ◆ The last sentence in the book is: "Such men don't grow on every bush." Explain what you think this means.

- ◆ What would have happened if the peasants did not bring the ingredients that the soldiers asked for as they were making the soup?

- ◆ Write a new story. Choose one of these titles: "Popcorn Soup," "Bubble Soup," "Feather Soup," "Rain Soup," or "Speckled Soup."

- ◆ Rewrite the story so that it takes place in the future. Who would the characters be? What foods would they bring for the soup? Where would they eat and sleep?

Ten Important Sentences

A summary is a shortened form of a story. It contains all of the important information that someone would need to know if he or she wanted to retell the story to someone else.

The ten sentences below tell the story of *Stone Soup*, but they are listed in a mixed up order. Cut out the sentences and arrange them in the correct order on another piece of paper. When you are finished, read your summary of the story to a friend.

The peasants thank the soldiers for teaching them how to make stone soup.

Three soldiers are tired and hungry.

The peasants bring a pot with water and build a fire.

The soldiers say that the soup would be even better if they added spices, vegetables, beef, and milk to the stones.

The soldiers say that they will make stone soup.

The peasants set a large table and have a feast for everyone.

The peasants say that they have no food.

The soldiers put stones in the pot to start the soup.

The peasants bring spices, vegetables, beef, and milk for the soup.

The peasants see the soldiers coming and hide their food.

Name _____

Organize the Story

Fill in the characters, setting, problem, and solution to help you organize the story of *Stone Soup*. Then draw a picture in each of the squares to go along with your writing.

Characters: _____

_____

_____

Setting: _____

_____

_____

Problem: _____

_____

Solution: _____

_____

_____

Name _____

Comparing Characters

Use the Venn diagram to compare the two main character groups from the story.

Write information about the soldiers in the soldiers bubble. Write information about the peasants in the peasants bubble. Then write information that is the same for both groups in the middle where the bubbles meet.

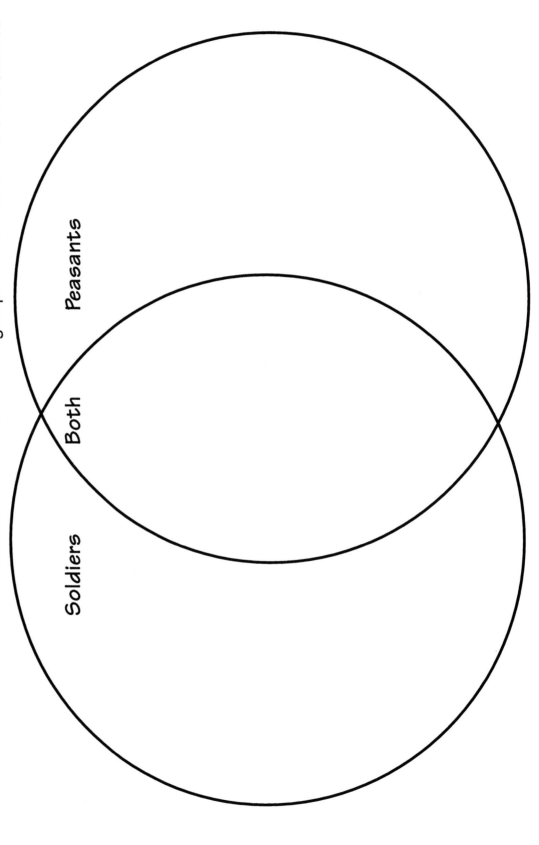

Peasants

Both

Soldiers

Plan a Soup

The soldiers in the story said that they could make soup out of stones. As they started to make the soup, they added other ingredients. If you were the soldiers, what would you put in the pot to start your soup?

Write your own recipe for soup on the recipe card. Then draw a picture of what your soup would look like in the pot below.

Strange Words

When Marcia Brown retells the story of *Stone Soup,* she uses some unusual expressions that you may not have heard before. An expression is a set of words, that when grouped together, have a special meaning. For example: She was *as fast as a rabbit.* This means that she was very fast.

Read the following expressions on the list below. Work by yourself or with a partner to explain what the expressions mean in your own words. When you are finished, compare your ideas with the class.

bit to eat	
none too large	
little enough for ourselves	
peasant's eyes grew round	
it's all in the knowing	
give them a send-off	
and fancy	

Why do you think the author chose to use these expressions when she wrote the story?

What are some unusual expressions that you have heard that may not be familiar to everyone in your class?

Same or Different?

An *antonym* is a word that means the opposite of another word. For example, *good* and *bad* are antonyms. Below are some words from the story *Stone Soup*. Match the words on the left with their antonyms on the right by coloring the matching set of antonyms the same color.

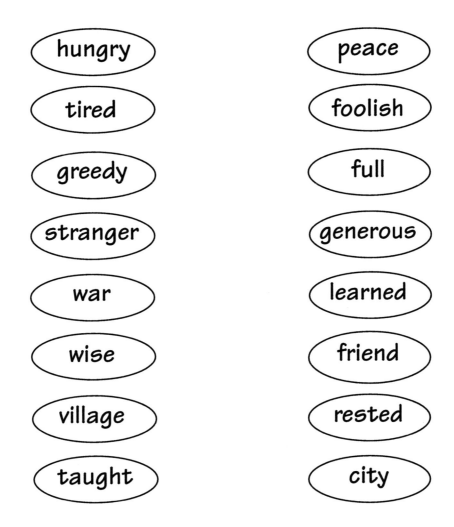

A *synonym* is a word that means almost the same as another word. For example: *small* and *little* are synonyms. A trick to help you remember what synonym means is that the words *synonym* and *same* both start with the letter "s". Write a synonym for each of these words from the story.

large _____   feast _____

village _____   trudged _____

soup _____   tired _____

What Do You Think?

Directions: Read the following quotation from *Stone Soup*. Then answer the questions below.

"Many thanks for what you have taught us," the peasants said to the soldiers. "We shall never go hungry, now that we know how to make soup from stones."

1. Do you think the peasants believe that soup can be made from stones?

   _____

   _____

   _____

2. Do you think soup can be made from stones?

   _____

   _____

   _____

3. Would the soup taste the same without the stones?

   _____

   _____

   _____

4. Do you think the peasants believe that the soup would taste the same without the stones? Why or why not?

   _____

   _____

   _____

5. Do you think the soldiers believe the soup would taste the same without the stones? Why or why not?

   _____

   _____

   _____

6. What did you learn about stone soup?

   _____

   _____

   _____

Best Beds

After they made stone soup, the soldiers were invited to sleep in the best beds in the village. One soldier slept in the priest's bed, one in the baker's bed, and one in the mayor's bed. Why do you think these were the best beds?

What would the best bed look like in your town? Whose bed would it be? Draw a picture of the bed in the house below. Then describe whose bed it is and explain why it is one of the best beds in your town.

_____

_____

_____

_____

Folk Tales Anyone?

The story *Stone Soup* is a folk tale. Folk tales are stories that are heard and remembered and then are orally passed on through generations. As a result, they often change a little with each retelling.

Try these activities with your students to help them understand the art of oral storytelling.

- Discuss how words and ideas can change as they are orally passed on from one person to another. Then play a few games of telephone to show how this can even happen to short sentences.

  Split the class into two teams and have each team make a line, sitting side by side on the floor. Whisper a short sentence to the first person at the head of each line. Have the students pass the sentence down the line by whispering it into the next student's ear. Have the last two students at the ends of the lines write down what they heard. Then read each team's sentence. Start with an easy sentence; then challenge your students with more complicated sentences, such as tongue twisters or silly riddles.

- Explain that folk tales also change as they are retold. Sometimes the storyteller wants to add more detail or forgets and changes part of the story.

  A good storyteller knows how to change his voice to make a story seem more real. He becomes louder or softer, changes his pitch or speed when different characters speak, and includes sound effects for emphasis. Split your students into pairs and challenge them to come up with voices to represent characters in different situations. Invite the pairs to share their voices with the class. Try the following.

  "Dinner will be ready soon." (scared mouse, grumpy bear, tired mom)

  "It is so cold outside." (old man, wet cat, sad child)

  "Where did I put my hat?" (angry wolf, happy woman, wiggly worm)

  "Get your boots on!" (frustrated teacher, giggly girl, stiff tree)

- For this activity you will need a tape recorder. A parent volunteer can also help time the students and keep the activity moving along. (You may also wish to use your parent volunteer to help you model the lesson before having the students begin their own team stories.)

  Explain to the students how folk tales are an oral tradition and that the folk tales they have read in class were probably told many times before they were written down and published in books. Then tell the students that they will be working in teams of three to tell their own folk tales. They will not be writing down their stories; instead, they will be telling their stories, orally, into a tape recorder. The stories will be played later for the class.

  After the teams are arranged, assign the students in each team to be responsible for telling the beginning, middle, or end of the story. Have each team choose a story title. Allow students time to plan their story ideas. As they are ready, have them sit in a quiet place to record their stories.

Story Ideas: Why does the skunk have a stripe? How did the giraffe get his long neck? Why does a cat purr? How did the owl become so wise? How did the raccoon get his two black eyes? How did the spider learn to spin a web?

Name_____

Math

Fraction Fun

Complete the vegetable and soup fraction problems below.

Color 3/6 of the vegetables green.

Color 2/6 of the vegetables red.

Color 1/6 of the vegetables blue.

Write the fraction that represents how many of each vegetable are in the soup pot.

carrots _____

potatoes _____

cabbage _____

broccoli_____

peppers _____

Color 3/4 of the soup bowls.

Color 2/6 of the soup bowls.

Color 1/5 of the soup bowls.

Color 7/8 of the soup bowls.

Soup Problems

A cook needs to plan ahead to make sure he or she will have enough ingredients to complete a recipe. Sometimes the cook needs to do some problem solving.

Solve the soup word problems from the story.

1. If it takes 19 carrots to make enough soup for the entire village and Francoise only has 16, how many more carrots will the peasants need?

    _____

2. If Marie has 14 cabbages, Francoise has 16 carrots, and Albert has 12 potatoes, how many vegetables do they have in all? _____

3. If 14 villagers have 2 bags of barley each, how many bags of barley do they have all together?_____

4. If each peasant could eat 2 cups of soup and there were 6 peasants, how many cups of soup would they need? _____

5. If it takes 3 cups of milk to make stone soup for 6 peasants, how many cups of milk would it take to feed 18 peasants? _____

6. If it takes 3 stones to make enough stone soup for 1 village, how many stones would it take to make stone soup for 4 villages? _____

Use this space to write your own food word problem. When you are finished, challenge a friend to solve your problem.

_____

_____

_____

_____

Counting in French

Stone Soup is a French folk tale. When the story was first told, it was probably told in French. Use the chart below to practice counting in French. Then work with a partner to make your own French counting book to share with the class.

Number	French Word	French Pronounciation
1	un	un
2	deux	doo
3	trois	twa
4	quatre	katr
5	cinq	sank
6	six	sees
7	sept	set
8	huit	weet
9	neuf	newf
10	dix	dees
11	onze	ohnz
12	douze	dooze

Graphing Ingredients

Graphing is a fun way to keep track of the ingredients in a recipe. Use the information from this paragraph to fill in the graph. Then use your graph to answer the questions written below.

The soldiers placed three stones in the soup. Children then brought one pepper shaker and one salt shaker. Francoise put in fifteen carrots. Marie ran home for three cabbages. Some other peasants brought eighteen potatoes and two sides of beef. Finally, the soldiers added four bags of barley and one cup of milk. The soup was delicious!

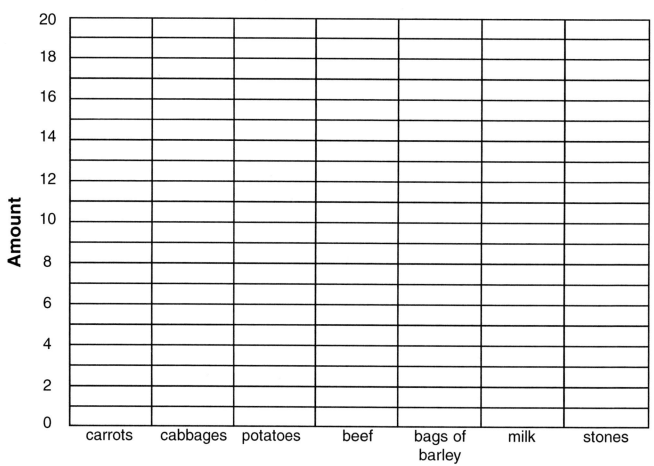

Soup Graph

1. What ingredient did the soldiers add the most of? _____

2. What ingredient did the soldiers add the least of? _____

3. What ingredients did the soldiers add the same amount of? _____

4. How many vegetables were added to the soup?_____

5. How many different kinds of ingredients were added to the soup?_____

Healthy Foods

The recipe for stone soup included ingredients from many different kinds of foods.

1. Make a list of all of the foods included in stone soup.

_____

_____

2. Make a list of the other foods served at the feast.

_____

_____

It is important that we eat the right amounts and the right kinds of foods every day. That way we keep our bodies healthy and strong. Study the chart below. It is called the food pyramid. It shows the kinds of foods you should eat each day and the number of servings you should have of each kind.

Food Pyramid
A Guide to Daily Food Choices

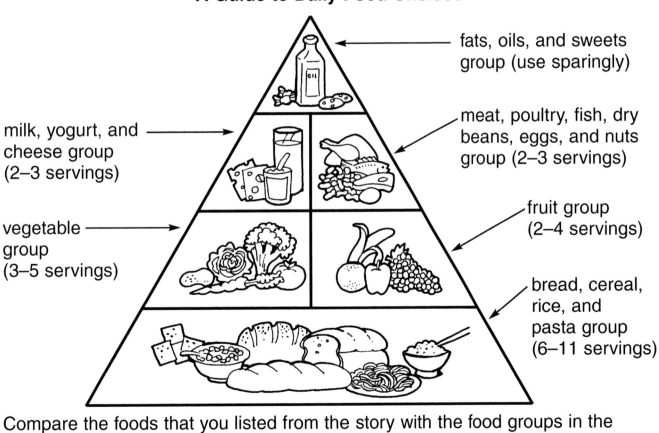

fats, oils, and sweets group (use sparingly)

meat, poultry, fish, dry beans, eggs, and nuts group (2–3 servings)

fruit group (2–4 servings)

bread, cereal, rice, and pasta group (6–11 servings)

milk, yogurt, and cheese group (2–3 servings)

vegetable group (3–5 servings)

Compare the foods that you listed from the story with the food groups in the chart. Did the peasants and soldiers prepare a healthy meal?_____

Would you add any foods to the feast to complete the meal? _____

If so, what would you add? _____

Healthy Foods *(cont.)*

Fill in the pyramid on this page with the foods you eat in one day. Be sure to write the foods in the correct sections. Share your pyramid with your classmates.

My Food Pyramid

fats,
oils,
and
sweets group
(use
sparingly) ———

milk,
yogurt, and
cheese group
(2–3 servings) ———

meat,
poultry, fish,
dry beans,
eggs, and
nuts group
(2–3 servings)

vegetable
group
(3–5
servings)

fruit group
(2–4
servings)

bread, cereal, rice, and pasta group (6–11 servings)

Do you think you are eating right? _____

What foods groups might you need to eat more of? _____

What food groups might you need to eat less of? _____

Smells

The peasants said that the soup smelled great and that they were very excited to try it. Our sense of smell helps us know more about our environment. We can smell things because we have tiny cells inside our noses. These cells send messages to our brains. Then our brains can tell us what we are smelling.

For this activity you will be testing your sense of smell. You will be working in groups of five. Each group will be given five different samples to smell. After you have smelled a sample, write down your guess as to what the cup contains. Write in your guesses below.

Sample 1	
Sample 2	
Sample 3	
Sample 4	
Sample 5	

Once you have tested all of the samples, compare your answers with your teammates. Then, open the cups to view the ingredients. Who has the best sense of smell? Which ingredients did you guess incorrectly? Were you surprised by any of the ingredients in the cups?

Teacher's Note: For suggestions on how to prepare the samples, refer to page 10.

Tastes

The peasants could not wait to taste the soup. When they tasted it, they said that it tasted so good that it was fit for a king. What kind of foods do you like to taste? Do you like sweet, sour, salty, bitter, or spicy foods? How do we know what different foods taste like?

Both our noses and our tongues help us to taste foods. When we smell a food, it makes the taste in our mouth seem stronger. Try this experiment to see how your nose can help you taste.

Experiment #1

You will need: banana, chocolate, peanut butter, cup of water

Pinch your nose closed with your fingers and take a bite of the banana. What do you taste? After a few seconds, release your fingers. Compare the taste before and after pinching your nose. Take a drink of water to clean out the taste. Then repeat the experiment with the chocolate and the peanut butter.

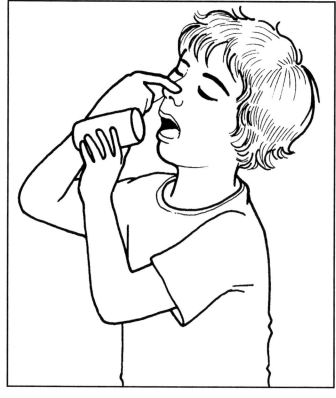

Did you notice a difference when your nose was unplugged?

How might your sense of taste change when you have a cold? Why?

Can you think of a time when not being able to taste something might be helpful?

Do you think this experiment would work with all foods? Why or why not?

Tastes *(cont.)*

The tongue is covered with tiny bumps called taste buds. These taste buds send messages to our brains to tell us what flavors the foods are that we are eating. We also have taste buds along the inside walls and at the back of our mouths. These taste buds also help us identify flavors.

We taste different flavors more strongly on different parts of the tongue. Sour flavors are tasted on the sides of the tongue. Sweet flavors are tasted on the tip or in the middle of the tongue. Salty flavors are tasted along the sides and toward the front of the tongue. Bitter flavors are tasted at the back of the tongue.

Try this experiment to test your taste buds.

Experiment #2

You will need: chocolate syrup, soy sauce, lemon juice, three Q-tips®, a mirror, and a cup of water

First, look at your tongue in the mirror. Notice the bumps. Do they change when you tighten or loosen your tongue muscle? Locate the back, middle, tip, and sides of your tongue so you will know where you are testing your samples.

Dip a Q-tip into one of the samples. Then, using the mirror to help you, touch the Q-tip to each of the four areas of your tongue. Make sure that you keep your mouth open until you are finished testing all four areas. Notice where the taste is strongest and where it is weakest. Rinse your mouth with the water, then repeat the experiment with each of the samples.

Where could you taste the chocolate syrup? The soy sauce? The lemon juice?

Compare your results with your classmates.

Where on your tongue might you be able to taste these foods best?

ice cream _____　　watermelon _____

popcorn_____　　soda _____

pickles _____　　potato chips _____

Hat Patterns

Your students can make these easy paper hats to wear as they perform reader's theater, make stone soup, or participate in a fun culminating activity.

Peasant Bonnet

Materials

- medium-sized paper bag
- ribbon or yarn
- scissors
- crayons, paint, or markers

Directions

1. Cut about 6" (15 cm) from the open end of the paper bag.
2. Open the bag and cut away the front face of the bag.
3. Fold the bottom of the bag up once or twice to make a cuff around the base of the bonnet. You may also fold the paper to form a cuff around the front of the bonnet that surrounds the face.
4. Poke holes in the paper at the sides of the bonnet and string yarn through.
5. Decorate the new hats!

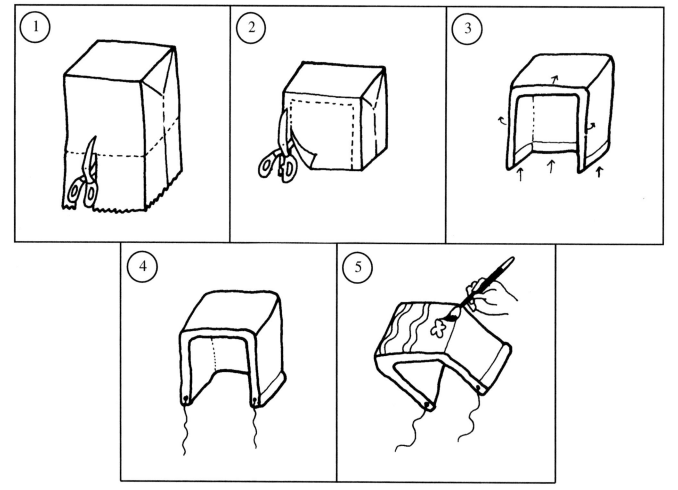

Hat Patterns *(cont.)*

Soldier Hat

Materials

- 2 sheets of newspaper
- tape
- crayons, paint, or markers
- feathers

Directions

1. Fold one piece of the newspaper inside the other and then hold the paper with the fold at the top.
2. Find the center and fold the top corners down and in to meet at the center. They should form two triangles.
3. Fold up two layers of the newspaper at the bottom to form a rim.
4. Flip the hat over and do the same to the back to form a rim. Tuck the end corners in to hold the rim in place. The hat should look like a large triangle.
5. Hold the two bottom corners of the triangle and open the hat so it looks like a cone. Bring the two corners together to meet in the middle and fold. Once this is done, the hat should look like a diamond.
6. Hold the hat with the creased edges at the top and the open edges at the bottom. Fold the top two layers of the bottom corner up to meet the top of the square. This will form a triangle on the front side.
7. Flip the hat over and repeat on the back.
8. Place a small piece of tape at the peak of the hat to hold it in place.
9. Open the hat and decorate!

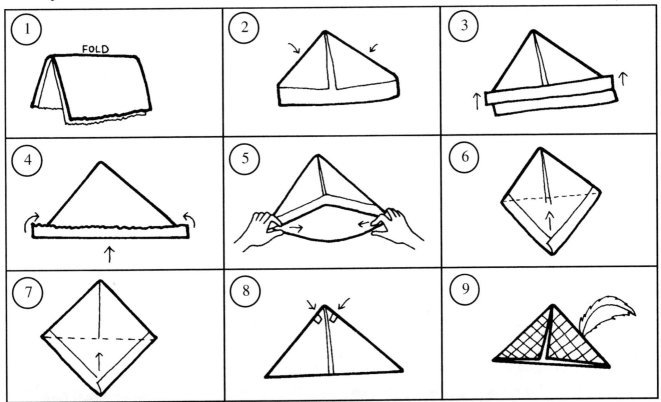

French Folk Song

After the feast, the peasants sing and dance to celebrate their new friendship and the marvelous food. Teach your students this simple French folk song, then combine it with the folk dance on the next page.

(*French*)	(*Pronounciation*)
Sur le Pont d'Avignon	**Sir ler Pon d'Avinyon**
Sur le pont d'Avignon On y danse, on y danse Sur le pont d'Avignon On y danse tout en round Les belles dames font comme ci Et puis encore comme ça Sur le pont d'Avignon On y danse tout en round	Sir ler pon d'Avinyon On ee danseh, on ee danseh Sir ler pon d'Avinyon On ee danseh toot on rond Lay bell daum fon com see Eh pweez oncore com sa Sir ler pon d'Avinyon On ee danseh toot on rond
Verse #2 This verse is the same except that the line about the belle dames is changed to Les monsieurs font comme ci	 Lay Messyur fon com see

♩ = 120 fast temp

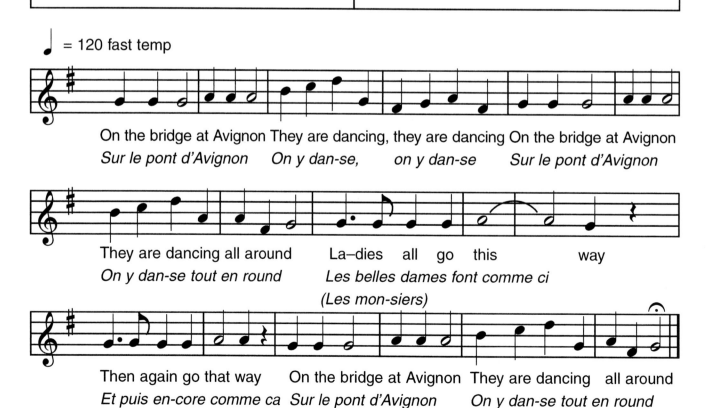

On the bridge at Avignon They are dancing, they are dancing On the bridge at Avignon
Sur le pont d'Avignon   On y dan-se,   on y dan-se   Sur le pont d'Avignon

They are dancing all around   La–dies   all   go   this   way
On y dan-se tout en round   Les belles dames font comme ci
(Les mon-siers)

Then again go that way   On the bridge at Avignon   They are dancing   all around
Et puis en-core comme ca   Sur le pont d'Avignon   On y dan-se tout en round

Folk Dance

Folk dances are usually a combination of a few simple steps that are repeated. They are often passed down through generations and are performed by the participants for self-entertainment at celebrations or gatherings.

This easy folk dance can be done with the entire class in one large circle, or with groups in smaller circles. The dance is designed to accompany the folk song on page 42. Each line of step directions corresponds to one line from the song.

Dancers start in a circle holding hands.

1. Take 4 steps around the circle to the right – counter clockwise.

2. Step in, feet together (swing arms up). Step out, feet together (swing arms down).

3. Take 4 steps around the circle to the left – clockwise.

4. Step in, feet together (swing arms up). Step out, feet together (swing arms down).

5. Girls step to the middle and walk in a counter clockwise circle with left arm held toward the center of the circle, making a star. Boys stand in place and clap to the beat.

6. Girls turn and walk in a clockwise circle with right arm held out toward the center of the circle, making a star. Boys stand in place and clap to the beat.

7. Girls step back into the group circle as everyone takes 4 steps to the right.

8. Step in feet together (swing arms up). Step out, feet together (swing arms down).

Repeat dance for verse two with boys stepping to the center to make a star.

Let's Make Soup

A fun way to culminate your unit on *Stone Soup* is to make soup. You may wish to take two days to complete this activity. Parent volunteers might also be helpful.

Writing About and Planning the Soup

Discuss recipes with the class. Make a list of all of the important parts of a recipe: the ingredients, the directions, how long the food needs to cook, how high the heat should be, and how many servings the recipe will make. Ask the students why each part of the recipe is important.

Then have students work in cooperative teams to write their own recipes for stone soup. Remind them to plan for a soup that will serve the entire class. Assign a gopher, a recorder, a reporter, and a director for each group. Have the students record their recipes on the recipe card outline on page 45. When the teams are finished, bring the class together and compare recipes.

Place the recipe that is written below on an overhead or on butcher paper and compare it to the recipes that the teams wrote. Discuss how the recipe only serves 10. Ask the class what they would need to do to make the recipe serve the entire class.

Tell the class that you will be making stone soup. You may want to assign students to bring in ingredients and materials needed to make the soup.

Recipe to use as a guide:

Ingredients

- 3 clean, smooth stones
- 1 pound (453 g) of beef
- 3 carrots
- 1/2 cup (118 mL) milk
- pepper
- 12 cups (2.8 L) of water
- 6 potatoes
- 1 cup (236 mL) of barley
- 1/2 cup (118 mL) chopped cabbage
- 1/2 tsp. (2.46 mL) salt

Directions

1. Bring the water to a boil.
2. Cut all of the ingredients into 1/2 to 1 inch-sized (1.3—2.54 cm) pieces.
3. Add the beef and the barley to the water. Lower to a simmer for about 45 minutes, stirring occasionally.
4. Check to see if the beef is almost cooked through.
5. Add the potatoes. Cook for about 10 minutes.
6. Stir in the carrots, cabbage, milk, salt, and a pinch of pepper.
7. Allow to simmer for another 10 minutes.
8. Serve in Styrofoam cups or small bowls with plastic spoons.

Cooking time: About 1 hour, 15 minutes

Serves: About 10

Writing a Recipe for Stone Soup

My Recipe

Recipe: _____

Ingredients: _____

_____

_____

_____

Directions: _____

_____

_____

_____

_____

_____

_____

_____

_____

Cooking Time: _____

Number of Servings: _____

Time to Prepare: _____

Souper Supper

One fun way to culminate your unit on *Stone Soup* is to hold a soup supper. After making stone soup with your class, invite parents or another class to come taste your masterpiece. Students can present their puppet shows, perform a reader's theater, or tell their own team folk tales. They can also teach the visitors the new folk dance and folk song. Samples of the students' work can be on display around the room, and a recipe collection book can be available at the front of the room.

You are invited to attend our Souper Supper!

Where: _____

When: _____

Come join us for a taste of stone soup
and some folk tale fun.

Bibliography and Related Resources

Other Books by Marcia Brown (a partial list—Caldecott Award books)

Cinderella, or The Little Glass Slipper. Aladdin Paperbacks, 1997.

Dick Whittington and His Cat. Aladdin Paperbacks, 1997.

Once A Mouse. Aladdin Paperbacks, 1989.

Shadow. Aladdin Paperbacks, 1995.

Counting Books

Baker, Alan. *Gray Rabbit's 1, 2, 3.* Kingfisher, 1999.

Carle, Eric. *The Very Hungry Caterpillar.* Putnam Publishing Group, 1984.

Hooker, Yvonne. *One Green Frog.* Grosset and Dunlap, Inc., 1999.

McGrath, Barbara. *The M&M Counting Book.* Charlesbridge Publishing, 1994.

Food Collection Agencies

Feed the Children
333 North Meridian Ave.
Oklahoma City, Oklahoma 73107-6568

America's Second Harvest
116 S. Michigan Ave., #4
Chicago, Illinois 60603
www.secondharvest.org

Related Web Sites

Homearts Network
http://homearts.com/depts/family/47cookf1.htm

Kids Food CyberClub
http://www.kidsfood.org/

Family Food Zone
http://www.familyfoodzone.com/fridge.html

Answer Key

Page 22

1. Three soldiers are tired and hungry.

2. The peasants see the soldiers coming and hide their food.

3. The peasants say that they have no food.

4. The soldiers say that they will make stone soup.

5. The peasants bring a pot with water and build a fire.

6. The soldiers put stones in the pot to start the soup.

7. The soldiers say that the soup would be even better if they added spices, vegetables, beef, and milk to the stones.

8. The peasants bring spices, vegetables, beef, and milk for the soup.

9. The peasants set a large table and have a feast for everyone.

10. The peasants thank the soldiers for teaching them how to make stone soup.

Page 27

hungry—full

tired—rested

greedy—generous

stranger—friend

war—peace

wise—foolish

village—city

taught—learned

Some suggestions for synonyms are as follows:

large—big, huge

village—town

soup—stew

feast—dinner, meal

trudged—walked

tired—sleepy, exhausted

Page 28

Answers will vary.

Page 31

Color 3 green, 2 red, and 1 blue.

carrots 2/10, potatoes 3/10, cabbage 1/10, broccoli 1/10, peppers 3/10

Color 3, 2, 1, and 7 bowls.

Page 32

Teacher's note—to modify the page for younger students, white out the 1's before copying. This will simplify the math.

	(with #1's)	(without #1's)
1.	3 carrots	3 carrots
2.	42 vegetables	12 vegetables
3.	28 bags	8 bags
4.	12 cups	12 cups
5.	9 cups	4 cups
6.	12 stones	12 stones

(or 3 if they carried the same stones to each village)

Page 34

1. potatoes

2. milk

3. cabbage and stones

4. 36 vegetables

5. 7 ingredients (9 with salt and pepper)

Page 35

1. Foods in soup: salt, pepper, carrots, cabbage, potatoes, beef, barley, milk

2. Foods at feast: bread, roast, cider

3. Yes, they served a healthy meal.

4. They could have added a fruit.